Dedicated to Children Everywhere

**Our future bathed in the
light of love is assured
because YOU are in the world!**

Cover Illustration by Stefan Keller
Logo Design by Sarah Miller

Hardcover ISBN 978-0-6450405-1-7
Paperback ISBN 978-0-6450405-2-4
Kindle e-Book AISN B08P1VSYJJ

First paperback edition Nov, 2020
Second paperback edition Jan, 2022

Paperback editions printed by Amazon
Hardcover printed by Barnes & Noble

First printing 2020

Published by
Earth Troopers
earthtroopers@hotmail.com
www.earthtroopers.com.au

NEW EARTH CHILDREN

AN A TO Z

BY Lehani Williams

ILLUSTRATIONS Stefan Keller
Angela Yuriko Smith
Enrique Meseguer
Beate Bachmann
Kai Stachowiak
Caroline Sattler
Alemko Coksa
Enrique Garre
Sarah Richter
Gerd Altmann
Okan Caliskan
JilV Martinez
Comfreak
Janrye

A is for **a**nswers:
there **a**re **a**nswers
in n**a**ture so connect
with E**a**rth d**a**ily

B is for **b**liss **b**u**bb**les: they are everywhere, jump on **b**oard!

C is for **c**ourage:
be **c**ourageous
for you are strong
and brave

D is for **d**reams:
follow your **d**reams,

they will lea**d** you
to magical places

E is for **e**volution: w**e** ar**e** **e**volving fast**e**r than you can imagin**e**

F is for faith: have faith
in the universe and have
faith in yourself

G is for **g**ratitude:
when we are **g**rateful,
more **g**ood things
can come

H is for **h**eart:
move to t**h**e r**h**yt**h**m of your own
heart, it knows exactly **h**ow to beat

I is for **i**mag**i**nat**i**on: **i**mag**i**ne the world you'd l**i**ke to l**i**ve **i**n, then watch **i**t come al**i**ve

J is for **j**oy: feel **j**oy... dance with it!

K is for **k**indness: this is the number one quality we must cultivate more of in this world

L is for **l**ight:
focus on the **l**ight,
be the **l**ight,
let it grow

M is for **m**indfulness:
be aware of **m**onkey **m**ind,
still your thoughts
and listen

N is for **n**ormality: whatever you do, do**n**'t try to be **n**ormal

O is for **o**pp**o**rtunity: there are d**oo**rs **o**f **o**pp**o**rtunity everywhere. D**o**n't be shy to **o**pen them!

P is for **p**atience: try
to be **p**atient and make
time to watch flowers grow

Q is for **q**uest:
don your armour,
and stand tall;

you're on a **q**uest to
never doubt yourself!

R is for **r**ainbow:
rainbows sp**r**ead thei**r**
love all ac**r**oss the wo**r**ld

S is for **s**tar**s**:
when you look to
the **s**tar**s** remember
the magic and
my**s**tery of the
univer**s**e

T is for **t**ru**t**h:
hear i**t**, speak i**t**, know i**t**,
you have your own **t**ru**t**h

U is for **u**nicorn: of co**u**rse they're real and don't let anyone tell yo**u** otherwise

V is for **v**isionary: see beyond, see far and wide, hold your **v**isions

W is for **w**orld: one **w**orld,
one love, **w**e are one

X is for **x**-ray goggles: look within people and see we're all the same

Y is for **y**ou: dare to be authenticall**y** and exquisitel**y** **y**ou!

Z is for **zzzzz**: get plenty of them, we have work and play ahead, Earth children

About the Author

Fremantle, western australia, is where Lehani has mostly called home.

Graduating from University in 2001, she taught ESL in south Korea & then primary school in places such as remote, indigenous australia & London, U.K..

New Earth Children, an A - Z, is Lehani's first published book. It was 'planted' in her mind during a beach walk, early in 2020. It then evolved with signs, such as, when undecided whether the letter 'f' should be about Fairies or faith, she asked for a sign from the universe & a car displaying the number plate 'faith' drove by.

Through this book, Lehani hopes to inspire the young reader with a sense of Universal Love & self belief as they embark on a journey of phonemic awareness.

In receiving & writing this book, she believes there are great lessons in divine timing & never allowing dreams to go to the land of lost dreams!

STEFAN KELLER

JANRYE

ENRIQUE GARRE

GERD ALTMANN

BEATE BACHMANN

ENRIQUE MESEGUER

SARAH RICHTER

ALEMKO COSKA

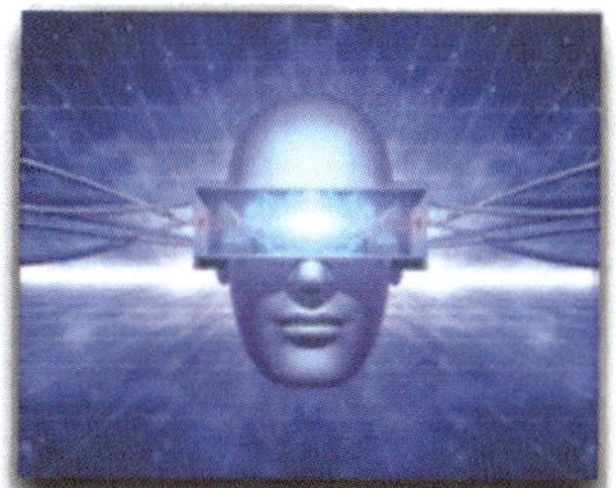

OKAN CALISKAN

COMFREAK

ANGELA YURIKO SMITH

JILV MARTINEZ

artists
via pixabay

Printed in Great Britain
by Amazon

86712345R00020